THINKING OUR WAY
THROUGH THE BIBLE

THINKING OUR WAY THROUGH THE BIBLE

Devotional Thoughts and Poems

JO ANN AND RUSS D. RHODES

XULON PRESS

Xulon Press
2301 Lucien Way #415
Maitland, FL 32751
407.339.4217
www.xulonpress.com

Unless otherwise indicated, Scripture quotations taken from the
Holy Bible, New International Version (NIV). Copyright © 1973,
1978, 1984, 2011 by Biblica, Inc.™. Used by permission. All rights
reserved.

Scripture quotations taken from the English Standard Version
(ESV). Copyright © 2001 by Crossway, a publishing ministry of
Good News Publishers. Used by permission. All rights reserved.

Printed in the United States of America.

ISBN-13: 978-1-63221-986-2

TABLE OF CONTENTS

Dedication

*To God
For His glory

*To our friends
You encouraged us with your joyful acceptance
of our Bible studies and poems

*To our parents, Ralph and Ruah, Joe and Elizabeth
You gave us shining examples of how to love God and His Word

INTRODUCTION

IT CAN BE EASY TO MISS THE LITTLE DETAILS IN Scripture. So often we gloss over phrases in an otherwise familiar verse or paragraph without putting thought into why that phrase is there or what the implications of those added details can be for our everyday Christian living.

There are lessons to be learned from those little details. All Scripture has been given to us in order to teach us how to live and walk in obedience to God's Word. By taking the time to think through those verses, we will find ourselves marveling at the wisdom God has passed on to us through His Word, as well as at the creative ways we can gain deeper understanding of what He has said.

This book is the product of God's Holy Spirit moving in our hearts and thoughts as we have spent time in His Word, thinking our way through it, so to speak, as we have read and meditated. God wants to speak to all of us and enable us to grow spiritually, and this book is a part of how He has done that in our personal lives. Most of the poems are reflections on the need to consistently grow stronger in one's Christian walk, hence the theme of fitness that the reader will notice in the poems throughout the book.

It is our prayer that each person reading this book will find that same blessing of learning and becoming more spiritually fit.

We invite you to think your way through the Bible with us!

Shut In

Genesis 7:16b
Then the Lord shut him in.

WHEN NOAH RECEIVED INSTRUCTIONS FOR building an ark, he probably did not understand all of what God was about to do. He had never experienced a flood of any kind, especially one like what was about to happen. However, the story of Noah shows us that he had a strong relationship with God. Genesis 6:9 tells us that Noah *walked faithfully with God.* Genesis 6:8 says he *found favor in the eyes of the Lord,* and Genesis 6:22 tells us he *did everything just as God commanded him.*

As a result of Noah's walk with God and his total obedience, God took care of him. Noah may not have understood the importance of closing the door in preparation for the flood, but that did not matter because God shut him in.

When God shut the door to protect Noah from the impending disaster, He was doing so in order to protect Noah. Only those who stepped through the door of the ark would be saved from the flood. Noah's protection came after he and his family obeyed God's command to build and then enter the ark. Their salvation from that flood came only as a result of their obedience.

The closed door of the ark was God's reminder to Noah that he was under God's protection. In those six little words, we can find courage and comfort: *Then the Lord shut him in.* The door is also our own reminder. Even when we face things that we could not know about or be prepared for ahead of time, God will shut us in. We will be safe. We will be secure. We do not have to know or understand everything in order to be kept safe. If we are walking with God and obeying Him just as Noah did, He will take care of the details.

Remember what Jesus Himself said in John 10:9: *I am the door. If anyone enters by Me, he will be saved.*

FIT 2 SUBMIT

Submission to God's sovereignty is
Believing without comprehending
Obeying without understanding
Going without knowing

(Genesis 12 and Hebrews 11:8)

THINK ABOUT IT

Is there a time when God shut you in as He did Noah? How did that make you feel secure?

Rainbow of Promises

Genesis 9:17
God said to Noah, "This is the sign of the covenant I have established between me and all life on the earth."

THERE WAS A PURPOSE FOR THE RAINBOW THAT God put in the sky after the flood. It was a sign. The rainbow was God's sign to all life of the earth, mankind as well as all the animals, of His promise to Noah and those who came after him that He would never again use a universal flood to punish sin.

People often do not keep their promises, but God always keeps His. Each color in the rainbow can represent a promise that God has made.

Red reminds us of God's love, which has no limitation. In John 3:16, Jesus says, *For God so loved the world that he gave his one and only Son, that whoever believes in him shall not perish but have eternal life.*

Orange reminds us of joy. God promises everlasting joy to the one who follows Him. Psalm 16:11 tells us, *You make known to me the path of life; you will fill me with joy in your presence, with eternal pleasures at your right hand.*

Yellow reminds us of the glory and spiritual light of God Himself. Psalm 27:1 says, *The LORD is my light and my salvation—whom shall I fear?*

Green reminds us of growth. If we follow and obey God, He promises us spiritual growth. 1 Peter 2:2 states, *But grow in the grace and knowledge of our Lord and Savior Jesus Christ.*

Blue reminds us of the peace God provides for those who trust Him. Isaiah 26:3 says, *You will keep him in perfect peace, whose mind is stayed on You, because he trusts in You.*

Indigo reminds us of wisdom. Who does not need some of that? Proverbs 8:10-11 says of wisdom, *Choose my instruction instead of silver, knowledge rather than choice gold, for wisdom is more precious than rubies, and nothing you desire can compare with her.*

Purple reminds us of royalty. Revelation 19:16 tells us, *On his robe and on his thigh he has this name written: KING OF KINGS AND LORD OF LORDS.*

FIT 4 PROMISES

O God, You are the
Great Promise Keeper

You promise
To never leave me alone
To help me keep pressing on
To lead me all the way home

You promise
To guide each step that I take
To keep me and never forsake
To answer the prayers that I make

You promise
To lift me whenever I stumble
To listen whenever I grumble
To help me when in deep trouble

You promise
To help me with my heavy load
To keep me on the narrow road
To lead me to Your safe abode

O God, thank You for
Keeping ALL Your promises

THINK ABOUT IT

What color of the rainbow is most meaningful to you personally?
What is your favorite promise from God?

Never Give Up

Genesis 24:15
*Before he had finished praying, Rebekah came out
with her jar on her shoulder.*

THERE ARE TIMES SUCH AS THIS SERVANT'S EXPERI-
ence when we have to pray and trust God for the answer to our
prayers. It often becomes obvious that God is answering our prayer
almost before we finish praying. Those answers to prayer serve as our
encouragement when we do not see immediate answers. Sometimes
God is even answering our prayers before we actually pray them. He
tells us in Isaiah 65:24, *It will also come to pass that before they call, I
will answer.* Before we complete our prayers, God begins to respond
to them, but other things may delay our ability to see His answers.

This servant's experience at the well is a vivid example of what
God can do for those who put their trust firmly in Him. He
always answers their prayers. Abraham had given his servant a big

responsibility, that of finding a wife for his son Isaac. The girl had to be from a family that the servant had not had contact with for many years, if ever. He had no way of knowing the potential wife for Isaac. All he could do was to ask God for a sign that he had met the "right" girl when that happened. Just think of how much stronger that servant's faith in God was after seeing that answer to his prayer, especially when he returned home to Abraham with the "right" girl and a story unlike anything he'd ever been able to relate before!

Keep praying, and don't give up! God won't fail to answer your prayers. Luke 18:1 says, *Jesus told his disciples a parable to show them that they should always pray and not give up.*

FIT 2 B MORE

If we were more alone with God
We would all know more of God
We would live more near to God
We would grow more in grace
We would walk more by faith
We would trust and obey more
And become more like the Lord
Whom we worship and adore

(Genesis 24:63)

THINK ABOUT IT

Write out in your own words how you think Abraham's servant related his experience to Abraham when he got home from his trip.

REASSURANCE

Genesis 46:4
*I will go down to Egypt with you, and I will
surely bring you back again.*

IN MANY WAYS, IT WAS NO DOUBT DIFFICULT FOR
Jacob to leave Canaan even though he was going to see his long-
lost son Joseph, who had been secretly sold into slavery by his older
brothers. Now, after many years, Jacob had learned of Joseph's mirac-
ulous rise out of slavery to become a high-ranking official in the
Egyptian government. As such, he was able to provide needed food
and shelter for Jacob's entire family during a destructive famine.

This meant, however, that Jacob would be leaving his long-time
home that was filled with special memories. He was such an old
man to travel so far, especially a trip of at least 650 miles that would
probably take at least several months to walk. There was a lot of
packing and planning he would need to do—his family was large.

More than that, Jacob had to leave his home in Canaan, the place God had promised to him through his grandfather Abraham, the place where his beloved wife Rachel was buried, and he knew he probably would never return.

All this made Jacob very nervous and not just a little frightened, so he turned to God. On the first stop of that long, arduous journey, Jacob turned to God for reassurance that he was doing the right thing. He offered sacrifices (the form of praying of that time) and heard a response from God. God reassured Jacob of His presence. *I am God, the God of your father, he said. Do not be afraid to go down to Egypt, for I will go down to Egypt with you.* That promise gave Jacob the courage to continue his trip even though he was not sure about how everything would work out.

When life becomes frightening because of the uncertainties that come along with no obvious outcome, we can turn to God and find peace in spite of the uncertainty. With that peace, we can move ahead into the uncertainty with confidence, just as Jacob did.

FIT 2 WIN

Go forward fearlessly
Stand strong triumphantly
Fight hard victoriously
Pray much expectantly
Run the race faithfully
Win the prize graciously

(Genesis 46:3-4)

THINK ABOUT IT

Think about a time when you faced an uncertainty about the future. What was uncertain about it? How did you handle your uncertainty?

What Do You Have?

Exodus 25:2b

You *are to receive the offering for me from everyone whose heart prompts them to give.*

AT THE TIME GOD GAVE MOSES THE TEN Commandments, He also gave him instructions for building a special place in which to worship. The materials for constructing that place (actually a tent) and its furnishings would come from offerings that the people of Israel would donate. Moses instructed them to bring from what they had, and each offering was to be brought by whoever was willing to donate something. Exodus 35:5 says, *From what you have, take an offering for the* LORD. *Everyone who is willing is to bring to the* LORD *an offering.*

God instructed Moses to tell the Israelites that they should bring offerings for use in building the tabernacle, but there was no further persuasion that Moses needed to give. Instead, God told Moses to receive the offerings that anyone brought. That was the entirety of God's instruction. Those who heard the request and whose heart prompted them to give would bring the offerings.

The result was nothing short of amazing. The offerings came continuously, freely given, morning after morning.

My offering to God should be the same. It can be as simple as a small act of kindness, a gentle response to a not-so-gentle comment, or a prayer of thanks to the Lord. Just make it continuous, freely given, and daily. God will bless what you bring, even if you think your offering is small or insignificant.

FIT 4 LIGHT BEAMS

Truth from our lips
Holiness in our life
Joy in our hearts
Knowledge in our heads
Love from our hands

All these are light beams
From the sacred light
Of God the Holy Spirit

May we never lack
Oil for this light
May it always last
All through the night
Amen and amen

(Exodus 25:6)

THINK ABOUT IT

What kinds of offerings have you recently brought to God? How has He blessed that offering? If you like to draw, draw a picture depicting your offering.

Blessing

Numbers 6:24-27
The Lord bless you and keep you; the Lord make his face shine on you and be gracious to you; the Lord turn his face toward you and give you peace. So they will put my name on the Israelites and I will bless them.

THIS BLESSING IS SO BEAUTIFUL! ALL BY ITSELF, IT has beauty and meaning, but the last sentence in verse 27 makes this blessing especially meaningful. God had instructed Moses to have Aaron the priest declare this blessing over the people, In doing so, Aaron was placing the name of God on them, which is what brought God's blessing upon them.

As His children, what is the result of having God's name on us?

God's name brings holiness. In the Bible, "to bless" means "to make or pronounce holy." That is what our faith in Christ as our Savior brings to us. We receive the name of God as well as the holiness that comes from being forgiven and freed from the power of sin. Colossians 1:22 tells us, *But now he has reconciled you by Christ's physical body through death to present you holy in his sight, without blemish and free from accusation.*

God's name brings protection. He keeps us. Psalm 121 tells us that God watches over us day and night.

God's name brings acceptance. He turns His face toward us. When a person turns their face toward another, what are they doing? They are showing that they are paying attention to what that other person is saying or doing. That is what God does to the one on whom His name rests. He pays attention to us.

God's name brings peace. In Him, we have spiritual peace. Romans 5:1 states, *Since we have been justified through faith, we have peace with God through our Lord Jesus Christ.* We also have lack-of-worry peace. Psalm 4:8 says, *In peace I will lie down and sleep, for you alone, Lord, make me dwell in safety.*

God's name is powerful and brings great blessing to each one who carries that name.

FIT 4 PEACE

The Preparation by the Lord
    He goes ahead of you
The Presence of the Lord
    He will be with you
The Provision from the Lord
    He will not fail you
The Peace of the Lord
    I will not fear

(Deuteronomy 31:8)

THINK ABOUT IT

How has God's name brought blessing to you? Give some examples
of the results of that blessing in your life.

Keeping Guard

Numbers 8:26

They minister to their brothers in the tent of meeting by keeping guard, but they shall do no service. [ESV]

RETIREMENT IS IN THE BIBLE! ACCORDING TO THE verses immediately preceding this one, the Levites, who were the ones God had chosen to serve as priests in the tabernacle, were to serve from age twenty-five to fifty, at which time, they were to retire.

The retirement of the Levites was not to be completely without responsibility. Instead, it was to be spent assisting, keeping guard. Keeping guard was a service to the other priests. In other words, retirement was not the end of the Levites' work. It was only a change of responsibility. These priests were still capable of doing something; it just was not the same "something" they had been previously doing.

So it is with my own retirement. I may not be doing the same thing I was doing during my younger years, but God still has something for me to do in my later years. When I begin to feel frustrated because I am not able to do much of those same things (I *am* getting older), this verse reminds me that I am not lacking a role to play...I simply have a *different* role to play.

That begs the question: what is my new task? The answer is right here in this verse. The retired priests ministered to their brothers by "keeping guard." I do not see this as my indication that I should become a security guard, but rather that I am to "keep guard." Prayer is my answer. Through prayer, I can help protect the church, its leaders, its members, and its ministries. By praying, I can also protect my family and friends. In keeping that responsibility in my retirement, I will be ministering to those for whom I am praying. I will be guarding them.

FIT 2 RETIRE

R Regular routines required no more

E Ending one phase of life
  Entering another with delight

T Treasured memories of
  Triumph in trial

I Incredible illustrations of
  Godly influencing

R Rejoicing in an uncharted future
  With resources from
  An unchanging God

E Encountering more challenges
  With less change

Enjoying more mess
With less stress

THINK ABOUT IT

Retired or not, over whom can you keep guard?

My Knight in Shining Armor

Deuteronomy 33:26
There is none like God...who rides through the heavens to your help, through the skies in his majesty. [ESV]

THESE FINAL WORDS OF MOSES BEFORE HIS DEATH capture one's imagination. Picture the classic dream of many a young girl, the dream of being rescued, swept off her feet by a knight in shining armor riding a white horse. That is exactly what I picture when I read this verse.

In my imagination, I am in need of help, and when I call out, my Knight in Shining Armor comes galloping across the heavens in all His majesty to rescue me.

I am like Little Red Riding Hood, who wandered off the path in the forest and, in doing so, met the big bad wolf. Isaiah 53:6 says, *We all, like sheep, have gone astray*. Little Red Riding Hood was rescued by the woodsman, who killed the wolf. Think about that for a moment...Jesus was a carpenter! *He saved us, not because of righteous things we had done, but because of his mercy* (Titus 3:5).

I am like Sleeping Beauty, asleep under the spell of sin. Ephesians 2:1 tells us, *You were dead in your transgressions and sins.* Sleeping Beauty was rescued by the prince who came looking for her, just as I was rescued by Jesus. *But because of his great love for us, God, who is rich in mercy, made us alive with Christ even when we were dead in transgressions—it is by grace you have been saved* (Eph. 2:4-5).

I am like Cinderella, for whom the prince searched the countryside. *For the Son of Man came to seek and to save the lost* (Luke 19:10).

When I needed rescuing from sin, I called out and my Knight in Shining Armor came galloping across the heavens in all His majesty to rescue me and give me salvation and eternal life. With Him, I will be able to live happily ever after.

In my daily life, when I am in need, I can call out to my Knight in Shining Armor, knowing He will come galloping across the heavens in all His majesty to help me.

What comfort to know how much God will do for me at any time, in any circumstance, whenever I call out to Him for help. God is my Hero, the One who rescued me from sin, the One who helps me in my daily challenges. He is my Knight in Shining Armor.

FIT 4 STRENGTH

Strength for each day
Grace for each need
Power for each duty
God gives to me

Love for the lost
Joy on the journey
Consider the cost
Christ died for me

Love for the sinner
Hate for the sin
God is Forgiver
Jesus within

His Holy Spirit
Comforter Friend
Helper Advocate
True to the end

(Deuteronomy 33:27)

THINK ABOUT IT

As a child, what was your favorite fairy tale? How can you relate that story to the reality of God's love or protection? How would you illustrate that love or protection in a drawing?

Take The Hill

Joshua 14:12

You yourself heard then that the Anakites were there and their cities were large and fortified, but, the Lord helping me, I will drive them out just as he said.

ALL THROUGHOUT LIFE, WE ALL FACE DIFFICULties, and the story of Caleb gives us a good example of how we can face those difficulties when they come along. Caleb worked with Moses when spying out the Promised Land and assisted Joshua in leading the Israelites as they conquered that land. Now, in this verse, he was asking for his "fair share," since, at the time, there was relative peace in the rest of the country.

How did Caleb face the challenge of the strong Anakites and their large, fortified cities? He faced the reality of the difficulty. He did not try to ignore the magnitude of what he was facing, nor did he ignore the fact that he was no longer a young man (he was eighty-five years old).

Our difficulties may look big, bad, or frightening, but we can do what Caleb did and trust God's promise of victory over difficulties. We can recognize that God will help us, even if we face something hard or something we have never had to face before. We can believe that God will help us, and we can rely on Him much more than our own natural strength and courage.

Caleb's secret is clear: he wholly followed the Lord God of Israel. He was totally committed to God and God's purposes in his life. Caleb had faith in the real and active presence of God and followed Him wholeheartedly, which gave him the confidence to face his difficult situation and take his hill.

FIT 4 THE HILL

Take the high hill
By His grace
For His glory
Run the race

Take the high hill
With His strength
For His glory
Win at length

Take the high hill
All thy days
For His glory
And His praise

(Joshua 14:12)

THINK ABOUT IT

What difficulty are you facing right now? How can you use Caleb's principles to face your challenge?

WHAT'S PAST IS PAST

1 Samuel 16:1

The Lord said to Samuel, "How long will you mourn for Saul, since I have rejected him as king over Israel? Fill your horn with oil and be on your way."

SAMUEL WAS A PROPHET, BUT HE WAS ALSO THE leader of the Israelites. They had high regard of him, but as he grew older and less able to lead, the people began asking Samuel to find someone to be a king over them. The Israelites wanted a leader like the leaders of countries around them that had kings as the head of their governments.

Although Samuel did not want to do this, the people kept insisting. Not knowing how to respond, Samuel prayed for wisdom about what to do. God's answer to him was clear: anoint a king to take over the leadership of the nation. God then lead him to Saul, a tall, handsome, humble man.

Samuel obeyed God and anointed Saul to be king of Israel. Because of that special connection Samuel had to Saul, Saul held a special place in Samuel's heart. He represented a time when Samuel had asked God for help and God had answered his prayer. For Samuel, Saul was a sign of God's guidance and help, a sign of his own obedience and the resulting blessing.

Now, Samuel had to set aside what was in the past and move on to new steps of obedience. King Saul had become very proud and had turned away from God, meaning he could not govern as he should, and as our verse tells us, God rejected him as king.

Samuel couldn't dwell on what was done in his past. God had a new task for Samuel that meant setting aside the past. Samuel had no idea what the result of his new step of obedience would be, but he had to put aside his mourning over what had already happened. He needed to obey his new directive from the Lord even though he did not know exactly how it would work out. Samuel was nervous and afraid. How could he follow this new directive? 1 Samuel 16:2 tells us, *Samuel said, "How can I go? If Saul hears about it, he will kill me."* God's response was, *I will show you what to do.*

Like Samuel, we cannot allow ourselves to become so comfortable with what is familiar that we miss the opportunity to move ahead. God has more things for us to learn, more ways for us to experience His presence and direction.

We do not have to be afraid, for God is with us.

We do not have to worry about what we will do, for God will show us each step of the way.

FIT 2 LEAD

Warm my heart
All day long
Stir my soul
Make it strong
Fill my mind
Keep it pure
Make me whole
Steadfast sure

Lead my feet
In Your way
Bend my knees
Help me pray
Move my legs
Forward march
Push on me
Give me starch

THINK ABOUT IT

Is there something you are holding on to from your past? If so, is it keeping you from moving forward spiritually? How do you need God's help to move on?

DON'T ASK FOR JUST A FEW

2 Kings 4:3
Go around and ask all your neighbors for empty jars.
Don't ask for just a few.

2 KINGS TELLS THE STORY OF A MOTHER WHO learned a valuable spiritual lesson and passed it on to her children. As a widow, her troubles were numerous. Her husband had been a good religious man (2 Kings 4:1 says he "revered the Lord"). Now, she had a big debt and no way to pay it. In fact, she was destitute (verse 2 says she had "nothing at all except a small jar of oil"). In addition, she was in danger of losing her sons, for if her debt was not paid, her sons could be taken away as slaves.

This mother did the only thing she could think to do: she went to the spiritual leader, Elisha, and asked for help. How could Elisha help? He wasn't rich either. He was "just" a prophet. But God gave him an idea. We get a glimpse of Elisha's faith in his advice to the widow: *Go around and ask all your neighbors for empty jars. Don't ask for just a few* (2 Kings 4:3).

What did the widow do? She left Elisha and shut the door behind her and her sons and gave them instructions for collecting jars. She trusted God's prophet, for she trusted God. She showed an example of faith to her sons. In faith, this woman poured, and dish after dish was filled. Still she poured, filling them all, and she kept on pouring. Imagine the impact this had on her sons!

I wonder what would have happened if the widow had been timid and had her sons gather only a few empty jars! It is obvious that her blessing would have been small. She would have still been blessed, but her blessing would have been small instead of life-changing, which was the income she gained for herself and her sons from selling all the oil.

Our blessings are only limited by ourselves because there is no limit to God's love. There is no limit to His power to bless us. He gives in overflowing measure, far beyond our expectations.

BURDENS AND BLESSINGS

Burdens can become blessings
Trials turned into triumph
Thorns can bring thanksgiving

Burdens thorns and trials
Come from the trusted treasure chest of
God's wise and wonderful will

(2 Corinthians 12:7-10)

THINK ABOUT IT

In your own words, describe what you imagine the widow said to her children when telling them of Elisha's directive. Then explain how you think they may have responded as she was filling the containers with the oil. Draw a table full of containers.

Only Twenty-Two

1 Chronicles 12:28
And Zadok, a brave young warrior, with 22 officers from his family...

THOSE WERE TURBULENT DAYS IN THE COUNTRY of Israel. King Saul went to war against the enemy and was killed in battle. Then David was made king over Israel and went to live in Jerusalem, the capital city. David's new army was made up of volunteers, and every day, new men showed up to serve.

Chapter 12 of 1 Chronicles contains a list of armed men who joined David for battle, a total of 340,622 battle-ready men. Each group is listed by where they came from, how many there were in that group, and what their skill was. For example, from Judah, carrying shield and spear, there were 6,800 men, and from Ephraim, brave warriors, famous in their own clans, there were 20,800 men.

There is one exception in the list. Zadok, a brave young warrior, came with twenty-two officers from his family. Why was Zadok listed and named specifically? Perhaps even though he came with only twenty-two men, he still came to fight, or perhaps it is because he was brave enough to come with the little he had to offer. Whatever the reason, it is clear that the little bit Zadok offered made a difference to God and to David, enough of a difference to make him worth noting by name in this list.

We can learn from Zadok's experience. It does not matter how much you offer to God; rather, the fact that you offer what you have is all that matters to Him. That is exactly what Romans 12:1 tells us: *Therefore, I urge you, brothers and sisters, in view of God's mercy, to offer your bodies as a living sacrifice, holy and pleasing to God—this is your true and proper worship.*

FIT 4 WAR

The battle is the Lord's
With steadfast foot and our strong hand
With dauntless heart we'll take our stand
The battle is the Lord's
With flaming zeal rush to the fray
The hosts of evil shall fly away
The battle is the Lord's

The battle is the Lord's you know
The battle is the Lord's
With our strong hand
We'll take our stand
The battle is the Lord's

The battle is the Lord's you know
The battle is the Lord's
With dauntless heart
We'll do our part
The battle is the Lord's

The battle is the Lord's you know
The battle is the Lord's
With sword and shield
We will not yield
The battle is the Lord's

(1 Chronicles 5:22)

THINK ABOUT IT

What do you have that you have hesitated to offer to God for His use because you thought it was too little or not good enough?

Take Little Bites

Nehemiah 3:23
Benjamin and Hasshub made repairs in front of their house; and
next to them, Azariah son of Maaseiah, the son of Ananiah, made
repairs beside his house.

THE TASK OF REPAIRING THE ENTIRE WALL AROUND
Jerusalem was without a doubt a huge job for these few exiles who
returned from Babylon to repair the city. Where do you start
repairing when everything around you needs cleaning up and repair?

Think back on your own experiences of facing a big clean-up at
home, or perhaps a major reorganization of a closet. Sometimes the
enormity of the task at hand is overwhelming, almost to the point
of despair. One can only imagine how big and discouraging this
might have been for these Israelites. The entire city—every building,
every street—needed repair.

What do you tackle first? How do you go about doing repairs when everything needs to be repaired? You do what these Israelites did. You take a small "bite" and start working! Each family repaired the small portion of the wall that was in front of their own house. When all put together, all the little portions turned into a big job that was completed.

I cannot be deterred from doing a little bit at a time. Whether working on a physical project, such as cleaning out a closet, or a spiritual project, such as clearing out the clutter in our lives that is keeping us from moving ahead spiritually, when we take a little at a time, we can see big results.

FIT 2 B BUILDING

Be Building
Yourselves now up
On your holy faith

Be Praying
In the Spirit
Each and every day

Be Keeping
Yourselves in step
With the love of God

Be Looking
For His mercy
On the road you trod

Be Helping
Just any one
Who may have doubts and fears

Be Rescuing
All those who
Need saving from the fires

(Jude 1:20-23)

THINK ABOUT IT

What big spiritual task are you facing? Write out a possible strategy of small steps that can help you tackle that task.

Mountains Moving

Job 9:5a

He moves mountains without their knowing it.

I WONDER HOW MANY TIMES GOD HAS ANSWERED a prayer or done a miracle in my life when I did not even know He was working. I cannot answer that, but I *do* know how many times when, looking back, I can see how He was at work. I can only imagine how many mountains God is moving on my behalf that I don't even know about.

Job faced a similar situation. He had many trials and discouragements, including the loss of his livelihood and the even more difficult loss of all of his children. However, even in his troubles, he recognized the power and wisdom of God and began to think about that power and wisdom. That is what brought him to this statement in verse 5. The phrase "without knowing it" in the original Hebrew language means "suddenly" or "unexpectedly." God moves mountains, as it were, before they are aware of it.

What is the mountain in your life, the thing that seems un-resolvable or un-fixable? Remember what this verse says. God removes mountains, and they do not know it. Even if they are really high, large, strong, or challenging, He removes them.

Job's conclusions as he pondered the wisdom and power of God can be found as you read through the rest of his story. For example, Job 23:10 says, *He knows the way that I take, when he has tested me, I will come forth as gold.* Although Job did not know what had brought all this trouble and sorrow, his confidence was that somehow it would all bring about a good result in the end. In another verse, Job 42:2, Job concluded, *I know that you can do all things; no plan of yours can be thwarted.* Even after suffering so much loss and going through periods of doubt, Job kept his faith in God.

God is in control! No matter what the mountain is, He can move it if He wants to. For now, I can rest in the assurance my faith in God's power gives me, and I can thank Him for all the unknown mountains He has moved or is moving, even those I do not yet know about.

FIT 2 B TRIED

God knoweth the way that I take
When He hath tried me
I shall come forth as gold
I shall come forth as gold
Why should I ever forsake
He's always beside me
I believe what He told
I shall come forth as gold

(Job 23:10)

THINK ABOUT IT

Think back on a time when you saw that God had worked in your life but you only recognized it after the fact. How did that experience strengthen your faith?

My Birth Certificate

Psalm 87:6

The Lord records as he registers the people, "This one was born there." [ESV]

WHEN I READ THIS VERSE, I IMMEDIATELY THINK OF my birth certificate. When I was born, the attending doctor filled out and signed the document, recording the time, place, and other details of my birth. That birth certificate has been my proof of who I am and of my rights of citizenship for my entire life. When I needed a passport, I had to show my birth certificate. When I recently got a new driver's license, I had to show my birth certificate. It has always been an essential document.

So it is with my relationship to God. At the time of my salvation, the Lord recorded my "birth," and now He can look back, so to speak, and see that on that specific date, at that specific time, and in that specific location, I gave my life to Him and was born again.

I cannot remember my physical birth. I was there, but the memory is not. However, that event is recorded on my birth certificate so even though I cannot tell you the specifics of it from memory, I know that I was born because I have the proof!

God knows all about my spiritual birth. He recorded it in His Book of Life, and that is what is important. Even if I do not clearly remember all the details of that birth, I have my "birth certificate," and that is my proof that I am His child.

FIT 2 B KNOWN

Known of God completely
My ups and downs
My all arounds
My thoughts and words
Behind before
Known of God completely

Known of God continually
In heaven or hell
He there doth dwell
If winged to the sea
He there doth lead
In darkest night
He's there with light
Known of God continually

Known of God compassionately
Formed from above
Knit together in love
Wonderfully made
Framed up my way
Ordained all my days
He's worthy of praise
Precious indeed
Thy thoughts unto me
As sand by the sea
When I awake
I am still with thee
Known of God compassionately

(Psalm 139:1-18)

THINK ABOUT IT

What details about your spiritual "birth certificate" can you fill in? List them here.

My Spacious Place

Psalm 118:5
When hard pressed, I cried to the Lord; he brought me into a spacious place.

SMALL AND COZY PLACES ARE OFTEN NICE, AND there are times when I like to be in a small space. However, there are some places I desire to be more spacious, like my kitchen work area or my craft area in my house. Thankfully, this verse says when I am faced with difficulty, God can bring me to a spacious place.

What kind of place is a spiritually spacious one? The remaining verses of this psalm give us some descriptions of this.

It is a place where God's presence is felt (verse 8). He is with me, so I am not afraid.

It is a place of security (verse 9) and enabling. God is with me and is helping me, so I can do anything I need to do.

It is a place of victory (verse 7). With God, I can have victory over whatever or whoever causes trouble to me spiritually.

It is a place of safety (verses 8-9). I can find refuge in God from the turmoil around me.

It is a place of steadiness (verse 13). Even when I am about to fall because of the pressure of life and circumstances, God helps me, and I am able to remain standing.

It is a place of salvation (verse 14) and a place of joy (verse 15). There is such great pleasure (joy) in being able to face difficult circumstances and challenges knowing God is with me!

It is a place of thanksgiving (verse 21). Giving thanks is a natural, normal thing when you see how God has helped or encouraged you in some way.

This spacious place is obviously a restful and enjoyable one. I am so thankful that my spiritual house has a "spacious place" in it!

FIT 2 TRUST THE LORD

It is better to trust in the Lord
Than to put confidence in man
It is better to trust in the Lord
And watch Him unfold His good plan

It is better to trust in the Lord
Than to put confidence in princes
It is better to trust in the Lord
Who always keeps His promises

Trust in the Lord
Stand tall for God
Hold forth the Word
Do what is good

(Psalm 118:8-9)

THINK ABOUT IT

Describe your personal spiritual spacious place. Are there other characteristics of your space that were not listed in this devotion?

CHANGE

Psalm 119:89
Your word, LORD, is eternal; it stands firm in the heavens.

CHANGE IS NOT ALWAYS EASY. IT CAN BE HARD ON us. As we grow older, we find it more and more difficult to deal with change, yet there are some things in life that never change.

God's Word never changes. *Your word, Lord, is eternal; it stands firm in the heavens.* Isaiah 40:8 says, *The grass withers and the flowers fall, but the word of our God endures forever.* Spend time in the Word of God, for it will ground you so that you can weather any changes that come your way.

God's faithfulness never changes. Psalm 119:90 says of God, *Your faithfulness continues through all generations.* We can commit ourselves, our children, our grandchildren, and yes, even our great-grandchildren to Him! *You, Lord, reign forever; your throne endures from generation to generation* (Lamentations 5:19). As Lamentations 3:23 and an old hymn of the church both put it: *Great is thy faithfulness.*

God's power and authority over all creation never changes. In Psalm 119:91, we read, *Your laws endure to this day, for all things serve you.* Think about it: the sun and moon maintain the same distances from earth as they always have, the sun rises and sets as it always has, and the list of amazing facts of God's unchanging world goes on.

In some things, change is inevitable. When we trust Christ as our Savior, old things pass away and all things become new. 2 Corinthians 5:17 tells us, *Therefore, if anyone is in Christ, the new creation has come: The old has gone, the new is here!* Once this change takes place, other changes will be almost inconsequential in comparison because we will appreciate the unchangeableness of God and His Word.

FIT 2 WIN

Forgetting behind
Straining before
Putting behind the past
Straining for what will last

Forgetting gone Pressing on
Forgetting gone Pressing on

This one thing I do
Forgetting what is behind
Straining for what's ahead
I press toward the goal
To win the great prize
Toward heavenly skies
In the Lord Jesus Christ

Forgetting gone Pressing on
Forgetting gone Pressing on

THINK ABOUT IT

Which of God's unchanging characteristics is the most meaningful to you? Why? How does that knowledge empower you to press on?

HEMMED IN

Psalm 139:5

You hem me in behind and before, and you lay your hand upon me.

THE PHRASE "HEMMED IN" CAN SOMETIMES HAVE A negative connotation of limitations for us, but in this verse, the sense of the word is more of protection and assurance. We are hemmed in on all sides ("behind and before").

The verse says "you hem me in," which reminds us that it is God and His powerful, security-enhancing presence that surround us. Psalm 125:2 tells us, *As the mountains surround Jerusalem, so the Lord surrounds his people.*

Sometimes it is our friends (godly men and women) who hem us in, who stand as a wall of protection surrounding us, helping us in times of need or encouraging us in difficult situations. *They [David's men] were a wall around us all the time we were herding our sheep near them* (1 Samuel 25:16).

God's love surrounds us, hems us in. Psalm 32:10 says, *[God's] unfailing love surrounds the man who trusts in Him.*

Angels surround us. Psalm 34:7 comforts us with this truth: *The angel of the Lord encamps around those who fear him.*

We have real-life examples of people who loved and trusted God, and they surround us. Their examples give us courage to face whatever we are going through. Hebrews 12:1 states, *We are surrounded by...a great cloud of witnesses.*

In other words, being hemmed in on all sides can be a very good thing! That knowledge comforts us. It makes us feel secure and safe in God's hands, reminding us of God's love and care for us. We are hemmed in behind and before.

FIT 4 HIS HAND

The hand of the Lord is
A hand of salvation
A hand of direction
A hand of provision
A hand of protection

The hand of the Lord is
A hand of covering
A hand of rejoicing
A hand of caring
A hand of embracing

(Psalm 37:23-24)

THINK ABOUT IT

What is hemming you in right now? How is knowing you are
hemmed in meaningful and helpful to you?

Use Your Walker

Proverbs 4:11-12
*I instruct you in the way of wisdom and lead you along straight paths.
When you walk, your steps will not be hampered; when you run, you
will not stumble.*

FOLLOWING GOD AND HIS WORD IS LIKE USING A
walker to get around. Why does a person use a walker?

You might use a walker in order to walk straight, rather than weaving
from side to side. In our spiritual life, God and His Word help us
walk a straight path that is pleasing to Him. Proverbs 14:11 tells us,
I instruct you in the way of wisdom and lead you along straight paths.

You could also use a walker to keep you from stumbling or falling.
Similarly, God's Word keeps us from stumbling or falling into sin
and sinful ways. Psalm 37:31 says of God's people, *The law of their
God is in their hearts; their feet do not slip.*

Many people use a walker to keep their feet and ankles secure while making their way from place to place. As we follow God, His Word gives us spiritual security. Psalm 18:36 states, *You provide a broad path for my feet, so that my ankles do not give way.*

You could even use a walker to help you get where you want to go. Trusting God gives us the courage to live our lives no matter where He takes us. In Proverbs 16:9, we read, *In their hearts humans plan their course, but the Lord establishes their steps.*

A walker is a dependable way to get around for the person who is otherwise unsteady on their feet. When we trust God, we can feel safe in Him. Proverbs 3:6 tells us, *In all your ways submit to him, and he will make your paths straight.*

For some people, a walker helps with standing up straight enough to take steps. We please God by following Him and the direction that He gives us in His Word. In Proverbs 14:2, He reminds us, *Whoever fears the Lord walks uprightly.*

God's Word is my walker for my spiritual life.

AS YOU GO

As thou goest step by step
I will open up the way
before thee. (Proverbs 4:12,
old Hebrew translation)

As you go, step by step
I will open up
The way before you
I will open up the way

As you pray, day by day
I will open up
The way before you
I will open up the way

As you walk, trust and obey
I will open up
The way before you
I will open up the way

As you serve Him every day
He will open up
The way before you
He will open up the way

(Proverbs 4:12)

THINK ABOUT IT

Why do you need a spiritual walker?

God's Tattoo

Isaiah 49:16
See, I have engraved you on the palms of my hands...

HAVE YOU EVER WRITTEN SOMETHING ON YOUR palm to remember it? Even if it does not get washed off, what you write will eventually wear off, but what is pictured in this verse from Isaiah is something more permanent. It is more like a tattoo. It is "engraved."

This verse tells us that God has "tattooed" the names of His children on the palms of His hands. By doing so, He is conveying certain messages to us.

I can imagine the kind of tattoo God might have. Maybe it is the word "LOVED" in a big heart, followed by your name. After all, Romans 5:8 tells us, *God demonstrates his own love for us in this: While we were still sinners, Christ died for us.*

Or His tattoo might be the word "MINE." In 1 John 3:1, we read, *See what great love the Father has lavished on us, that we should be called children of God!*

Perhaps God's tattoo would include the word "CHANGED" with a butterfly. 2 Corinthians 5:17 says, *If anyone is in Christ, the new creation has come: The old has gone, the new is here!*

How about "FOREVER" as God's tattoo? In Revelation 3:5, He declares, *I will never blot out the name of that person from the book of life...*

Or maybe it is "MY TREASURE," as it is referenced in Deuteronomy 14:2: *Out of all the peoples on the face of the earth, the Lord has chosen you to be his treasured possession.*

God's tattoo reminds us of His love and mercy toward us. It shows us that if we have given our hearts to Him, we belong to Him. God's tattoo illustrates that He loves us and cares for us forever. It is permanent. We are engraved on His hands.

FIT 4 ME AND THEE

The Lord created me and thee
The Lord redeemed me and thee
The Lord called me and thee
The Lord reconciled me and thee
The Lord remembers me and thee
The Lord delights in me and thee
The Lord spares me and thee
The Lord is patient with me and thee
The Lord honors me and thee
The Lord rewards me and thee

(Isaiah 43:1)

THINK ABOUT IT

Can you think of more "tattoos" that would represent how God feels about you? Design your response as a tattoo.

"Make Like a Tree and Leave"

Jeremiah 17:7-8

Blessed is the one who trusts in the Lord, whose confidence is in him. They will be like a tree planted by the water that sends out its roots by the stream. It does not fear when heat comes; its leaves are always green. It has no worries in a year of drought and never fails to bear fruit.

THE PICTURE OF THE TREE BY THE WATER IS A VIVID description of the work God wants to do in the life of His child, making it a life of productivity and faith. During this life on earth, the blessing God wants to give us if we trust Him is like the description of the fruitful tree in these verses.

God wants us to be "planted" near Him, the source of Living Water. Having our spiritual roots reaching out for that Living Water produces some very good fruit.

With God, we will have the fruit of courage, for the tree planted near water does not fear even when there is heat.

We will also see fruit of consistency in our living, and our leaves will always be green. Remember, green leaves are a sign of life within!

The tree planted near the water will have the fruit of peace. It has "no worries in a year of drought." Even when drought is all around it, this tree will continue to drink from the water available.

When planted near the source of this Living Water, we will be productive. We will never fail to bear fruit.

These fruitful blessings are based on how far we send out our roots to get the Living Water we need to maintain our spiritual life. Only if we have planted ourselves near the streams of Living Water will we will never need to worry about growing dry, shriveling up, and being spiritually unproductive.

Whoever drinks the water I give them will never thirst. Indeed, the water I give them will become in them a spring of water welling up to eternal life. John 4:14

I AM SOWING

I AM GROWING:
The Seed has been planted
The soil has been watered
The SON has been shining
The Spirit has been moving

I AM GLOWING:
The joy of the Lord is my strength
The love of the Father is my hope
The Word of God is my confidence
The Peace of the Spirit is my comfort

I AM GOING:
The way of the cross leads home
The road to reward is soon
The walk on earth is steady
The home in heaven is ready

I AM SOWING:
The day is bright
The time is right
The Word is sure
The results secure

THINK ABOUT IT

What benefit(s) to being planted close to the Living Water is (are) the most meaningful to you?

Always

Zephaniah 3:17
The Lord your God is with you, the Mighty Warrior who saves. He will take great delight in you, in his love he will no longer rebuke you, but will rejoice over you with singing.

THIS VERSE IS A BEAUTIFUL DESCRIPTION OF THE relationship God has with me as His child.

He is always present. Psalm 139:7 says, *Where can I go from your Spirit? Where can I flee from your presence?* His presence brings joy to us, as Psalm 16:11 states, *You make known to me the path of life; you will fill me with joy in your presence.* God's presence gives us courage to face life. *If God is for us, who can be against us?* (Rom. 8:31).

He is always powerful. Isaiah 63:1 says, *He is mighty to save,* which tells us His power provides our salvation. According to Romans 15:13, His power gives us hope: *May the God of hope fill you with all joy and peace as you trust in him, so that you may overflow with hope by the power of the Holy Spirit.*

He is always passionate. *He will take great delight in you.* God loved us before we loved Him. 1 John 4:10 tells us, *This is love, not that we loved God, but that He loved us and sent his Son as an atoning sacrifice for sin.* God's love provided our way of salvation and eternal life because He was passionate about us.

He is always providing peace. *He will quiet you with his love.* When I feel discouraged, God encourages me. Romans 15:5 says, *May the God who gives endurance and encouragement give you the same attitude of mind toward each other that Christ Jesus had...*

He is always pleased with me. *He will rejoice over you with singing.* 1 Samuel 15:22 asks, *Does the LORD delight in burnt offerings and sacrifices as much as in obeying the LORD? To obey is better than sacrifice, and to heed is better than the fat of rams.*

In other words, when I am God's child, God is always present, always powerful, always passionate, always providing peace, and always pleased with me.

FIT 4 HIS SONG

The Lord your God is always here
The Lord is a warrior who wins
He rejoices over you with song
He will refresh you with His love

He's here
He wins
He sings
He loves

(Zephaniah 3:17)

THINK ABOUT IT

What aspect of God's relationship to you is most meaningful and encouraging for your Christian walk? Why?

Satisfied

Matthew 14:20
They all ate and were satisfied.

MATTHEW, MARK, AND LUKE ALL RELATE THE account of the feeding of thousands from just a small amount of food. One phrase is found in all three accounts: *They all ate and were satisfied.* When Jesus miraculously multiplied the food, making it available to the crowds, they did not just get enough to tide them over until they could get their own food. They had enough to be satisfied. For those in the crowd, there was no lingering need or desire for more than what they had received.

When we put our full trust in God and His love for us, we will find ourselves feeling so satisfied, so fulfilled by what He has spiritually provided for us that we will not need or want to search elsewhere. Psalm 90:14 says, *Satisfy us in the morning with your unfailing love, that we may sing for joy and be glad all our days.*

A strong relationship with God through Jesus gives us fulfillment that we do not see in many around us who are struggling with life. When this satisfaction principle is at work in one's life, it is not because that person has "arrived" at some kind of perfection or has had a life without its challenges. No, it is the fact that they have found satisfaction in knowing God and living close to Him. *All ate and were satisfied.*

FIT 2 B FULL

The fatness of thy house
The fountain of full life
The river of thy pleasure
The brightness of thy light

How excellent how excellent
Thy lovingkindness O God

(Psalm 36:8)

THINK ABOUT IT

What has made your relationship with God satisfying to you?

Lessons From an Unknown Man

Matthew 26:18-19

Go into the city to a certain man and tell him, "The Teacher says, 'My appointed time is near. I am going to celebrate the Passover with my disciples at your house.'"

ONE OF THE MOST WELL-KNOWN EVENTS LEADING up to the crucifixion, the Last Supper, took place in the home of a totally unknown person. Who was that "certain man"? His name is not mentioned in the Bible, but what is immortalized in this story is not *who* he was, but rather *what* he made available for Jesus' use.

Actually, we can learn a lot about this man from the biblical accounts of this event. He must have been a friend or follower of Jesus because he understood the disciples and made no further inquiries as to who the "Master" was when they referred to Jesus with that term. He had some kind of relationship to Jesus.

This man had a big house. It had an upper room that was large enough to accommodate Jesus and His disciples. He was also generous, for he was willing to let them use the room.

How long did it take this man to prepare the room for Jesus' use? The account tells us that he immediately responded. He had that room ready so that whenever it might be needed, he could make it available as soon as the request came.

God will use what I make available for His glory and His service. It will not be possible for me to be ready to give or serve "immediately" without already having a prior relationship with Jesus. Only then will my "room" be ready for His use.

FIT 2 B READY

Toes pointed in a heavenly direction
Hands folded for a heavenly connection
Tongue ready for a heavenly inspection
Mind ready for a heavenly correction
Soul ready for a heavenly injection
Body ready for a heavenly protection

THINK ABOUT IT

What did the unknown man teach you about being ready for God to use? Describe how ready you are.

DIVERSITY

Mark 2:14

And as he passed by, he saw Levi the son of Alphaeus sitting at the tax booth, and he said to him, "Follow me." And he rose and followed him. [ESV]

JESUS' TWELVE DISCIPLES WERE QUITE A DIVERSE group. Although they may have been diverse in background and ability, they were all alike in the reason Jesus appointed them, out of the many who were His followers, to be His disciples. In Mark 3:14, we read that Jesus appointed these men in particular to be with Him and to send them out to preach.

So, who were these twelve men? While we do not know a lot about many of the disciples, the gospels give us some clues about most of them. They were working men. Peter, Andrew, James, and John were fishermen.

We know that Matthew, also called Levi, was a tax collector. In Jesus's day, tax collectors were despised, regarded as traitors to their own people.

Simon the Zealot's name tells us that he was part of a political group. Zealots engaged in politics and anarchy in hopes of instigating a revolution that would one day overthrow the Roman government.

Philip, James, and Judas (not Judas Iscariot) were most likely tradesmen or businessmen of some kind. However, we know nothing of the livelihood of Thomas, Bartholomew (Nathanael), or Judas Iscariot.

This was quite a diverse group of men! Two of them were definitely "outsiders." Judas Iscariot was from the "south" (Judah), while all the others were from the "north" (Galilee). Levi (Matthew) was a tax collector. A good Jew would not even associate with tax collectors in private life, but here was Levi in this group of "good Jews."

I would love to have been a proverbial fly on the wall when Levi joined Simon, Andrew, James, and John in the group of men whom Jesus asked to join in His ministry! Yet in the gospels, nothing is ever said to make us think there were any big objections to Levi being a part of the group. Nor do we have any indication of Levi responding negatively to joining a group of people he could have considered beneath his social status as a tax collector.

Why was there so little objection to these "outsiders" joining? Their focus was on following and working with Jesus, which eliminated any social differences from causing trouble within the group. Let us likewise allow our desire to love and serve God together overcome all else. If we do so, we can change the world just as those disciples did.

FIT 4 MONEY AND THE MASTER

We may think that money

Gives you peace
Provides your food
Pays your bills
Grants you shelter

Offers reliable transportation
Provides a wonderful retirement
Finds the best doctor
Extends your life
Surrounds you with friends

But money competes with God
Promising the same
Faith in money is worthless
Faith in God is priceless
Trust His holy name

(Mark 12:41-44)

THINK ABOUT IT

What do you imagine went through the disciples' minds when Levi (Matthew) joined the group? How do you think God helped their reasoning so they were able to accept Levi?

Unable

Mark 6:5

He could not do any miracles there, except lay his hands on a few sick people and heal them.

WHEN JESUS WAS VISITING HIS HOME TOWN OF Nazareth, the response of the town population to Him was cool, which is surprising in many ways. Since He had grown up in that town, they knew Him, so they had to have known how upright and good He was. Even so, they took offense at him. The word "offended" means "scandalized." Think about it—Jesus was like a scandal to His town! The townspeople admitted to His supernatural abilities and acknowledged His wisdom (see Mark 6:2), yet they were scandalized by Him!

What follows is one of the saddest verses in the Bible, verse 5. Here was a man wise enough to be capable of teaching the people in the synagogue, a man able to do miracles (which they had mentioned), but He was unable to do miracles for the people of His own hometown.

One must wonder what those unbelievers in Jesus' hometown missed because of their unbelief. This makes me wonder if I have ever kept God from working in my own life. How could I do such a thing?

One time when I show unbelief is when I say, "My problem is not important enough to bother God about this." How big does a problem have to be? The answer is found in Luke 12:24: *Consider the ravens: They do not sow or reap, they have no storeroom or barn; yet God feeds them. And how much more valuable you are than birds!*

In other words, there is no problem too small to take to God and to trust Him for.

Another way I show unbelief is when I say, "I'll take care of it on my own." Here again, we see an answer to this in Scripture. Proverbs 3:6 says, *In all your ways acknowledge him, and he will make your paths straight.* In other words, God can and will help us when we put our trust in Him. Anything else could make God unable to do miracles in our lives.

FIT 4 POWER

Obey the voice of God
   Enjoy the power of God

Obey the voice of God
   Take heed
Enjoy the power of God
   Know healing

(Mark 3:5)

THINK ABOUT IT

How have you kept God from being able to meet your needs? How will you avoid this problem in the future?

Astonished or Afraid

Mark 10:32

They were on their way up to Jerusalem with Jesus leading the way, and the disciples were astonished, while those who followed were afraid.

YOU ARE PROBABLY FAMILIAR WITH THE "GOOD news vs. bad news" scenario. We often hear it used in jokes and humorous skits. However, there is a more serious side to the use of good news vs. bad news. Studies have been done on the effect and use of this scenario in business situations, such as informing an employee about the elimination of his position.

Jesus used this same technique in Mark 10:29-30. Notice what He told His disciples: "The good news is that you can follow Me and receive great blessing. There is some bad news because to follow Me, you may have to endure persecution. However, there is good news! Your blessings will be eternal."

It is very interesting to note the disciples' responses in verse 32 to what Jesus said. They were amazed, but those who followed behind responded with fear. Two groups of people saw and heard the exact same things, yet they responded in almost totally opposite ways!

What an interesting picture of response to God's Word and work. Sometimes what a child of God finds spiritually amazing, astonishing, or invigorating is the source of fear, anger, or mockery for those who do not believe. What the child of God finds encouraging and empowering in God's Word seems limiting or backward to spiritual naysayers.

What is the underlying reason for this drastic difference of response to the same message in this passage from Mark? That difference is based on one's relationship to Jesus and God's Word. A committed person is one who has voluntarily taken the action of commitment and is willing to make sacrifices to keep their relationship with Christ strong. Those who are just followers, on the other hand, are interested from a distance...without a strong commitment.

FIT 2 FEED AND FOLLOW

You are to feed your soul
God will follow your situation
You run to reach the goal
God will bring you His salvation

Following faithfully the Heavenly Father
Keeping step with the Holy Spirit
Joining hands on the job with Jesus

(Colossians 3:1-3)

THINK ABOUT IT

Which category of Christ follower are you, a disciple or a follower? Are you amazed at God's Word to you, or are you fearful? Explain.

Properly Dressed

Luke 12:35

Be dressed ready for service and keep your lamps burning.

HOW DO YOU GET READY FOR THE DAY EACH morning? Regardless of what they will be doing, one important step for everyone is getting dressed. Being properly clothed is a key for whatever job one will be doing, and this is the picture we get from this verse.

What does it mean to be properly clothed in a spiritual sense? To be clothed in the salvation that Jesus has provided. Isaiah 61:10 says, *I delight greatly in the Lord; my soul rejoices in my God. For he has clothed me with garments of salvation, and arrayed me in a robe of his righteousness.*

There are some other items in our spiritual wardrobe that we should wear. We have a garment of praise, for instance. Isaiah 61:3 tells us that we have *a garment of praise instead of a spirit of despair.* And there is also a garment of humility. 1 Peter 5:5 states, *Clothe yourselves with humility toward one another.* We have compassion we can wear, as Colossians 3:12 says, *As God's chosen people, clothe yourselves with compassion, kindness, humility, gentleness and patience.*

Have you noticed that the way you dress is not just for yourself? It is also for others. We want to look good and pleasing to those who see us, and how we are spiritually dressed will make a difference in the lives of other people as well.

To be well-dressed, we additionally need the right accessories, and the Bible gives us good "fashion guidance" on that. We all need a belt of Truth (Ephesians 6:14), shoes of Peace (Ephesians 6:15), and a light that is lit (Psalm 119:105: *Thy Word is a lamp to my feet and a light to my path*).

With our clothing on and our accessories in place, we will be ready to live a life pleasing to God, ready to serve Him when opportunities arise to show joy, compassion, and kindness to others.

FIT 2 WATCH

Your loins girded
Your lights burning
Like men waiting
God comes knocking
Finds you watching

(Luke 12:35-37)

THINK ABOUT IT

Describe how you are spiritually dressed and ready for service. What are you "wearing"? For you artists, illustrate your response.

Knowing and Understanding

Luke 24:45
Then he opened their minds to understand the Scriptures. [ESV]

FOR THREE YEARS, THE DISCIPLES HAD SPENT almost all their time with Jesus, watching Him and being exposed to His teaching, but they still had not grasped much of the essence of who He was or what He had been teaching. In a sense, their minds were still caught up in the training that had been taught in the Jewish traditions, which they had carried from their childhood as Jewish children.

But here, after Jesus' death and resurrection, as they sat in a room together, Jesus opened their minds, and they were ready to not only *know* but *understand* what they knew.

There is a difference between knowing something and understanding it. The disciples are certainly not alone in that experience.

For example, we can know what the Bible says, but we do not always understand what God wants us to learn from it. Only God can give us the ability to understand what we know.

We must continue to learn, to ask God to give us understanding. That is the key to constant spiritual growth that goes beyond just knowing a few facts from stories in the Bible. As we allow God to open our minds to understand the Scriptures, we will become more able to serve Him, just as what happened to those disciples.

Now the disciples were ready for whatever future plans God had for them, and we will be as well.

FIT 4 TREASURE

Where your treasure is
There will your heart be also
There will be your time
There will be your talents
There will be your mind

Make your treasure
Doing God's pleasure
With your talents and time
Give Him the best of your mind
And the prime of your time

Give God your talents and time
Your treasure too
Your testimony of what the Lord
Has done for you

Your talents – the gifts and abilities
On loan from God
Your time – to worship and
Serve Him and others
Your treasure – investments and money
And what you buy
Your testimony – telling others your story
Giving God the glory

(Luke 12:34)

THINK ABOUT IT

What is something that you know but need help in understanding?
Write a prayer asking God for help.

PLEASE BE SEATED

John 6:11
Jesus then took the loaves, gave thanks, and distributed to those who were seated as much as they wanted.

IN THIS VERY FAMILIAR STORY OF JESUS FEEDING the five thousand, there is a fact that is frequently overlooked but contains a very valuable spiritual lesson. Jesus and His disciples distributed the bread and fish to those who were seated. They did not give it to those who were wandering around, not to people standing on the fringes of the group, and not to the skeptics standing apart from the group.

Before the people received any of the food, Jesus had them sit down. By doing so, He created order rather than chaos. Every person who was seated was ready to receive a part of the food being distributed, and they would be ready to eat what was handed to them. It would be much easier for the disciples to distribute the food if everyone was seated.

By following that order, the people showed their expectation that something was going to happen. They must have sensed that Jesus was going to do something. Even though they did not yet know what He was going to do, they were willing to obey Him in anticipation.

What can we learn from this? As we spiritually sit quietly, listening for the voice of God, we will hear from Him. We hear God's still, small voice in our quietness before Him, not in the hustle and bustle of activity.

In order to receive the spiritual food that will give us the energy we need to live for God's glory, we must take time to sit, listen, and watch for the next step. As we sit quietly, God will provide the peace, the comfort, and the wisdom that we need for whatever is happening in our lives.

FIT 4 WAITING

When harried
And hurried
We end up hurting
Ourselves and others

Waiting for God
To bring things
About
This can
Give you reason
To shout

Waiting
And waiting
Often brings
More blessing

THINK ABOUT IT

Are you seated? Are you listening? Is there a person God is using to help "feed" you? Explain why you answered these questions the way you did.

The Way

Acts 24:14

I admit that I worship the God of our ancestors as a follower of the Way, which they call a sect.

THE APOSTLE PAUL SPOKE OF "THE WAY" IN THIS verse. "Way" refers to how someone works to attain a goal. That is important to understand as we think about what Paul stated concerning his faith in Christ. "The Way" is a description of how Paul was living and attaining his goal in life. He was following Christ, living a life pleasing to God.

How does the Bible describe "The Way" that Paul said he was following?

The Bible says this is the way of salvation. Jesus Himself gave insight into "The Way" in John 14:6, when He stated, *I am the way, and the truth, and the life. No one comes to the Father except through me.*

Proverbs 16:25 tells us, *There is a way that appears to be right, but in the end it leads to death.* Jesus is the only Way to salvation, peace, and eternal life, and to reach it, we must walk in The Way.

"The Way" is the way for good direction, i.e., guidance for doing God's will. All throughout the Bible, God promises us guidance. In Psalm 32:8, He says, *I will instruct you and teach you in the way you should go; I will counsel you with my loving eye on you.* Again, in Isaiah 30:21, we read, *Whether you turn to the right or to the left, your ears will hear a voice behind you, saying, "This is the way; walk in it."* There is only one Way to obey God and do His will, and that is to listen for His voice to your heart and then obey it.

This is "The Way" of protection. Psalm 18:30 says, *As for God, His way is perfect: The Lord's word is flawless; he shields all who take refuge in Him.*

When we follow "The Way" we will attain our goal of living a life pleasing to God just as the Apostle Paul did.

ENJOYING ENLARGEMENT

Psalm 4:1-8

Vs.1: Thou hast enlarged me when I was in distress
    I will be in distress
    God's **process** for growth
ENLARGEMENT – stretching
    I will be stretched

Vs.7: Thou hast put gladness in my heart
    I will be glad of heart
    God's **provision** for joy
ENJOYMENT – rejoicing
    I will be glad

Vs.8: Thou...makest me dwell in safety
    I will sleep in safety
    God's **protection** for life
CONTENTMENT – resting
    I will be safe

THINK ABOUT IT

How does following "The Way" affect you in your Christian walk?
Is it similar to or different from how Paul described it? If you like
to illustrate things in artistic form, try illustrating "The Way" in
a picture.

Up

1 Corinthians 14:3

But the one who prophesies speaks to people for their strengthening, encouraging and comfort.

AS A REPRESENTATIVE OF GOD AND HIS LOVE TO the world around me, there are some things that I can do to bring His Word alive for the people I come in contact with. I can follow the example God has set for me in what He has done for me as His child.

My words and demeanor should build up others. What I say can be used, in the words of this verse, *for their strengthening*. What does this mean? It means helping others to grow stronger in their faith. This is what God does for us. In Isaiah 41:10, He tells us, *So do not fear, for I am with you; do not be dismayed, for I am your God. I will strengthen you and help you.* This is what we should do for one another. For example, Acts 15:32 says, *Judas and Silas said much to encourage and strengthen the believers.*

My words should lift up others. I can encourage others. In what way should I encourage? I should encourage others to be more diligent to follow God's leading in everything and to keep their faith strong. In the Old Testament, Moses gives us a good example of this: *But charge Joshua, and encourage him, and strengthen him* (Deuteronomy 3:28). This is what we should do for one another. 2 Corinthians 12:11 states, *Strive for full restoration, encourage one another, be of one mind, live in peace. And the God of love and peace will be with you.*

My words should cheer up others. I should bring comfort to them through what I say. The word "comfort" implies the need for consolation and compassion, the need for support. It implies a burden of some kind. This is what God does for us. He comforts us, cheers us up. Isaiah 49:13 says, *Shout for joy, you heavens; rejoice, you earth; burst into song, you mountains! For the Lord comforts his people and will have compassion on his afflicted ones.* This is what we should do for one another. 2 Corinthians 1:3-4 expresses God's compassion, saying, *Praise be to the God and Father of our Lord Jesus Christ, the Father of compassion and the God of all comfort, who comforts us in all our troubles, so that we can comfort those in any trouble with the comfort we ourselves receive from God.*

FIT 2 PRESS ON

Every minute of the day
Every inch of the way
God holds your hand
And helps you stand
As you travel on
To the Promised Land

Every second of time
As you make your climb
Through the valley deep
Or the mountain steep
God holds your hand
And guides your feet

Every day of the year
As the time draws near
Toward your heavenly home
No longer to roam
Seeing Christ the King
On His glorious throne

Refrain:
Minute second day of life
Soon will end the battle strife
Victory won through Christ the Son
But 'til then keep pressing on

THINK ABOUT IT

List some ways in which you have built up, lifted up, or cheered up someone recently.

Win the Prize

Philippians 3:10-14
I want to know Christ...not that I have already...arrived at my goal, but I press on...toward the goal to win the prize...

PAUL'S GOAL WAS TO BECOME LIKE JESUS. HOW DID he do that? According to these verses in Philippians, he pressed on to take hold of that goal, straining toward that goal. He wanted desperately to reach it. We know this because Paul mentions three times how hard he was working toward that goal.

Paul was determined. He says he was pressing on toward the goal. What does "press on" mean? To press on means to continue moving forward while implying that there is some kind of resistance. It means that the person pressing on is determined! Jeremiah 29:13 says, *You will seek Me and find Me, when you search for Me with all your heart.*

Paul concentrated on his goal. He said he was forgetting what was behind in order to attain his goal, always straining toward it. Track and field athletes do that same thing when standing at the starting line for a race. You can see them concentrating, picturing what it will take to get to the end of the race. You can see every muscle strained and taut as they are waiting to take off, concentrating all of their energy on that task, not paying much attention to the crowd around them.

Paul anticipated reaching his goal. His mind's eye was like the athlete's eyes, fixed on the goal line in anticipation of getting there successfully. He wanted to run the race to the finish. After all, the whole reason for running the race is to finish! Hosea 6:3 tells us, *Let us acknowledge the Lord; let us press on to acknowledge him. As surely as the sun rises, he will appear; he will come to us like the winter rains, like the spring rains that water the earth.* To acknowledge is to recognize the authority, validity, or claims of someone or something. When we press on, straining toward God (acknowledging Him), we will find refreshment in our spirits.

We can reach the goal and win the prize if we stay determined.

FIT 4 ACTION

ACTION prayer plan

A **Adoration:** worship and enjoy being in God's presence
C **Confess** your sins and faults to God
T **Thanksgiving:** thank God for who He is and for what He does
I **Intercession:** pray about the needs and burdens of others
O **Observation:** look and listen for God's good orders to obey
N **Notation:** note where you now need to move out in God's plan

THINK ABOUT IT

What is your ultimate spiritual goal? What actions are you taking to help you concentrate on and achieve that goal?

Peace and Thankfulness

Colossians 3:15
Let the peace of Christ rule in your hearts...you were called to peace.
And be thankful.

WE ARE CALLED TO PEACE AND THANKFULNESS.
For what will peace make us thankful? We can find numerous
answers to that question throughout God's Word.

We are thankful for God's love. Being thankful for His love will
enhance your peace. Psalm 107:8 says, *Let them give thanks to the
Lord for his unfailing love and his wonderful deeds for mankind.*

We are thankful for salvation and eternal life made available to us
through Jesus' sacrifice for us. 1 Corinthians 15:57 declares, *Thanks
be to God! He gives us the victory [over sin and death] through our
Lord Jesus Christ.*

We are thankful for God's Word. In Psalm 119:62, the psalmist writes, *At midnight I rise to give you thanks for your righteous laws.*

We are thankful for Christian friends. 2 Thessalonians 1:3 tells us, *We ought always to thank God for you, brothers and sisters.*

We are thankful for answered prayer. Psalm 118:21 states, *I will give you thanks, for you answered me.*

Peace and thankfulness go hand in hand. When we are thankful for the blessings mentioned throughout God's Word, our peace will grow.

BE THANKFUL

Be careful for nothing
        In nothing be anxious, my friend
In everything give thanks, in everything give thanks
        For this is God's will in Christ Jesus

Chorus:

Be thankful be thankful be thankful my friend
Be thankful be thankful again and again

Be thankful He hears you
        In nothing be doubtful, my friend
He hears and He answers, He hears and He answers
        For this is God's promise and this is His plan

Be grateful He gave you
        His Spirit to comfort and guide
He never will leave you, He never will leave you
        Forever He will walk by your side

Be joyful, be joyful
        The joy of the Lord is your strength
Sing and rejoice, give thanks and sing
        Let us give praise to the King of Kings

(Philippians 4:6)

THINK ABOUT IT

What are you thankful for? How does giving thanks for those things enhance your peace?

TRAINING

1 Timothy 4:7
Train yourself to be godly.

GODLINESS DOES NOT COME NATURALLY FOR US. Even though I am a born-again child of God and have the Spirit of God at work in me, because of my sinful nature, I still have the constant battle against sin. This verse reminds me that I have to train myself to live in a godly fashion, to live a God-honoring lifestyle.

Paul does not say to "be godly" but rather to "train yourself to be godly." That phrase means exercising, as one who is training in a gym. Picture an athlete, who is continually exercising his joints and muscles so as to keep supple and to become stronger and better at his sport.

A typical professional athlete trains five to six hours a day, six days a week. Training isn't all fun and games! The same is true of spiritual "training." Hebrews 12:11 tells us that *no discipline seems pleasant at the time, but painful. Later on, however, it produces a harvest of righteousness and peace for those who have been trained by it.*

Good training includes all the parts of one's body, such as the feet and legs. That means walking according to God's Word and in love. 2 John 6 states, *And this is love: that we walk in obedience to his commands. As you have heard from the beginning, his command is that you walk in love.*

Our arms and hands also need to be strengthened with exercise, even for spiritual training. In the Bible, prayer is pictured in the raising of one's hands and arms toward heaven so strengthening one's arms and hands indicates increasingly powerful prayer. Hebrews 12:12 says, *Strengthen your feeble arms and weak knees.*

No good training program is complete without cardio exercise. One's heart must be strong. Deuteronomy 6:5 reminds us, *Love the LORD your God with all your heart and with all your soul and with all your strength.*

The reason for this diligent training is found in verse 8: *For physical training is of some value, but godliness has value for all things, holding promise for both the present life and the life to come.*

We need to train ourselves to be godly. Train every day of every week, every week of every month, and every month of every year. Doing so will make us strong, and it will enable us to win our race of life, life now and in the life to come.

FIT 2 LEARN A LOT

Moses learned a lot
In the palace of the king
He learned a whole lot more
In the desert of the King of kings

Jonah learned a lot
As a prophet with a wish
He learned a whole lot more
In the belly of a fish

Samson learned a lot
As a Nazarite he scorned
He learned a whole lot more
As he was grinding out the corn

Peter learned a lot
And he wanted more to know
He learned a whole lot more
When he heard the rooster crow

Martha learned a lot
Working cooking serving meat
Mary learned a whole lot more
Sitting still at Jesus' feet

In the desert of the Lord
Or the belly of a whale
Maybe grinding out the corn
It is best just to be still

THINK ABOUT IT

Describe God's training program for you.

Choose the Right Bank

1 Timothy 6:20a
Guard the deposit entrusted to you. [ESV]

HOW CAN WE GUARD THE DEPOSITS GOD HAS given us, His blessings of this life and of eternal life? By using our spiritual bank, of course! Jesus Himself spoke of spiritual banking. In Matthew 6:19-21, He tells us that we should lay up—or deposit— our treasure in heaven, where nothing can destroy it.

If a person wants to make certain their investments are safe and secure, what do they do? They deposit those investments in a good bank. Experts tell us that there are several principles involved in making the right choice of an investment bank. Those same principles are true for our spiritual banking as well. What should one look for in a good spiritual bank?

A good bank is insured. You want to make sure your money is safe. John 6:37b says, *Whoever comes to me I will never drive away.* The word "never" is our insurance that if we deposit our lives in God's bank, they are insured.

We want to find a bank that has reasonable fees, one that charges low fees and a minimum of them. According to John 3:16, our only spiritual "fee" is faith. In other words, this bank has very low fees!

When choosing a bank, we look for good customer service. As a client, we want to feel valued by our financial institution, so look for a bank that makes efforts to address your needs in a timely manner. What kind of "customer service" does God's bank have? John 14:13-14 gives the answer to this: *And I will do whatever you ask in my name, so that the Father may be glorified in the Son. You may ask me for anything in my name, and I will do it.*

Customers of a good bank look for high yield options. They want more for their money. God's bank offers very good options for just a small investment of faith. Romans 10:9-10 explains, *If you declare with your mouth, "Jesus is Lord," and believe in your heart that God raised him from the dead, you will be saved. For it is with your heart that you believe and are justified, and it is with your mouth that you profess your faith and are saved.*

Put your deposit in God's bank and reap the benefits. Deposit your life and receive salvation. Deposit your cares and receive peace. Deposit your concerns and receive joy.

EVERY MINUTE OF THE DAY

Every minute of the day
Every inch of the way
God holds your hand
And helps you stand
As you travel on
To the Promised Land

Every second of time
As you make your climb
Through the valley deep
Or the mountain steep
God holds your hand
And guides your feet

Every day of the year
As the time draws near
Toward your heavenly home
No longer to roam
Seeing Christ the King
On His glorious throne

THINK ABOUT IT

What characteristics most attract you to God's bank? Try drawing an "advertisement" for God's bank.

Get Your A.U.G. Degree

2 Timothy 2:15
Do your best to present yourself to God as one approved, a worker who does not need to be ashamed...

GRADUATION IS ONLY AVAILABLE TO THE PERSON who has met the requirements of a course of study and has passed an exam that proves that person has adequately learned the lessons of the course.

Our lives are much the same. As God's children, we are preparing for our "graduation" to heaven. We are working on our A.U.G. (Approved Unto God) degree!

What courses are required for this spiritual graduation? They turn out to be quite similar to what a high school student must study in order to graduate.

Literature/Language Arts is required. By studying God's literature (the Bible), we learn what pleases God, which equips us for living our lives in a way that pleases Him. 1 Timothy 3:16 says, *All Scripture is God-breathed and is useful for teaching, rebuking, correcting and training in righteousness.*

The study of Mathematics is also necessary. Psalm 90:12 reads, *Teach us to number our days that we may gain a heart of wisdom.*

Science is important as well. Psalm 8:3-4 asks, *When I consider your heavens, the work of your fingers, the moon and the stars, which you have set in place, what is mankind that you are mindful of them, human beings that you care for them?*

It is also necessary for us to study History. God never changes, so all that we learn of Him in the Bible, which was written hundreds of years ago, is still true today. Hebrews 13:8 tells us, *Jesus Christ is the same yesterday and today and forever.*

Economics is another important subject. In Matthew 6:19-21, Jesus says, *Do not store up for yourselves treasures on earth, where moths and vermin destroy, and where thieves break in and steal. But store up for yourselves treasures in heaven, where moths and vermin do not destroy, and where thieves do not break in and steal. For where your treasure is, there your heart will be also.*

Another required course of study is Government/Civics. Jesus instructs in Matthew 22:21, *Give back to Caesar what is Caesar's, and to God what is God's.*

Physical Education is usually included in a high school curriculum, and we find it in the spiritual school as well. Hebrews 12:2 says, *Let us run with perseverance the race marked out for us, fixing our eyes on Jesus.*

FIT 4 BIBLE STUDY

Things 2 look 4

    Knowledge of God
    What do we learn about God?

    Promise 2 Claim
    What promise is there to claim?

    Command 2 Obey
    What command is there to obey?

THINK ABOUT IT

What subjects do you need to study a little harder before you can earn your own A.U.G. degree?

A Special Memorial

Hebrews 12:1-2

Therefore, since we are surrounded by such a great cloud of witnesses, let us throw off everything that hinders and the sin that so easily entangles. And let us run with perseverance the race marked out for us, fixing our eyes on Jesus, the pioneer and perfecter of faith.

ALMOST EVERYONE CAN NAME SOMEONE THEY admire, someone who has inspired them in some way, whether a living person or a person from history. We often honor these people through memorials. A memorial is a way of preserving the memory of a person or thing.

These verses in Hebrews speak of a "memorial" of sorts, a "great cloud of witnesses." Who are these witnesses? They are all the saints of the Old Testament, whose lives testify to the power of faith. They stand looking on us, as it were, in our struggling, running, wrestling, and fighting. They are encouraging us, having shown us examples of faith in God and His Word.

What are they witnesses about? They have proven that you can have confidence in God. He will always be with you to help you and sustain you in any and every situation. They witness to the fact that God will give you the grace and strength to bear whatever circumstances or situations you face in your life. They are also witness of the fact that God keeps His promises to His children.

How many witnesses are there? Hebrews tells us there is a "great cloud." This includes anyone who has lived before us who trusted God and walked with Him. One day, we will be part of that cloud of witnesses for the generations that come after us.

However, notice that verse two explains that we are not to place our main attention on those witnesses. Our eyes are to be fixed on Jesus, because it is from Him that we draw our strength and courage to follow the example of those witnesses. When we do that, we are creating a special memorial to the faith of those who had faith before us.

FIT 2 RUN

Throw off everything that hinders you
Run with perseverance your race
Fix your eyes on Jesus
Consider Him who endured
Then you won't lose heart and quit

Throw it off – (simplify)
Run your race – (persevere)
Fix your eyes – (meditate)
Look to Him – (encouragement)
Do not quit – (obedience)

(Hebrews 12:1-3)

THINK ABOUT IT

Who is in your cloud of witnesses? What would they tell you if you could speak with them now? What would you tell them?

Hurl Those Cares

1 Peter 5:7
Cast all your anxiety on him because he cares for you.

THIS VERSE TELLS US TO CAST ALL OUR ANXIETY ON God. The word "cast" means to throw or hurl something. Understanding that gives us a very picturesque understanding of just what God wants us to do with whatever is worrying us.

If I throw something, it ends up quite far away from me. Likewise, if I hurl an object, I am throwing it as hard as I can, with great force. In other words, I do not lay the object down nearby, where I can pick it up again easily. If I have hurled it, then I have to consciously and actively go find it and pick it up. This means I have to take action concerning my anxieties, actively hurling them at God, where I do not have to try to pick them up again.

This verse also tells us what anxieties we are to cast upon God. God wants us to cast all our cares on Him. We are not only to cast the large things or the small things, but *all* things. How much is "all"? It is everything. After we cast our anxieties on Him, nothing will be left for us to worry about!

Notice also that this verse says we cast all of our ("your") cares on Him. That is, all the very personal cares or anxieties that we face in our personal lives, whether real or imagined. 2 Corinthians 10:5 says, *Casting down imaginations...and bringing into captivity every thought to the obedience of Christ.* Therefore, we are to cast all our personal anxieties on God.

Why does God want you to do this? Because "He cares for you." To care about someone means to fix your thoughts on them. In other words, we cast our anxieties on God because He is always thinking about us, His children.

Let's make wise plans in all areas of our lives, make the decisions we need to make, and at the same time, refuse to allow ourselves to be strangled with worry concerning things we cannot control. Let's hurl our worries at God!

Psalm 55:22: *Cast your cares on the Lord and he will sustain you; he will never let the righteous be shaken.*

FIT 4 HIS CARE

Thank You, LORD, for
Your loving watch care
Your caring protection
Your protecting guidance
Your guiding provision
Your providing salvation
Your saving grace
Your gracing forgiveness
Your forgiving love
Your loving favor
Thank You
Thank You
Thank You, LORD
Now and forever

THINK ABOUT IT

What care or worry do you need to "hurl" at God? Write that care or worry on a separate piece of paper, wad it up into a ball, and hurl it across the room. As you walk over to pick it up, consider the offer God has made for you to hurl that care or worry at Him instead of carrying it around.

Follow the Recipe

2 Peter 1:5-8

For this very reason, make every effort to add to your faith goodness; and to goodness, knowledge; and to knowledge, self-control; and to self-control, perseverance; and to perseverance, godliness; and to god-liness, mutual affection; and to mutual affection, love. For if you possess these qualities in increasing measure, they will keep you from being ineffective and unproductive in your knowledge of our Lord Jesus Christ.

HAVING EFFECTIVE AND PRODUCTIVE FAITH IS LIKE baking a cake. To be successful at baking, you must follow the recipe. If you want your recipe to turn out, you cannot leave out any ingredients.

In the recipe for effectiveness and productivity, the key ingredient is faith. Just as you cannot make many cakes without flour, likewise, faith is an essential ingredient for this spiritual recipe. This verse says to "add to your faith," the assumption being that you have the faith that you want to increase.

There are some other ingredients needed for your spiritual cake. What do you add to your faith? First of all, you must add goodness (moral excellence, kindness, generosity). Ephesians 4:32 tells us, *Be kind and compassionate to one another, forgiving each other, just as in Christ God forgave you.* After that, add in some knowledge (knowing the right thing to do). Proverbs 1:7 reminds us, *The fear of the Lord is the beginning of knowledge.*

Next, add self-control (choosing to do the right thing even when it is difficult). Then put in some perseverance (steady persistence in a course of action, especially in spite of difficulties; always doing the right thing). In Luke 21:19, Jesus talks about the end times, saying, *Stand firm, and you will win life.*

These verses say to add godliness (doing the godly thing, living a godly life) and mutual affection (doing the kind thing). Romans 12:10 says, *Be devoted to one another in love.* And finally, include love (doing the loving thing) in the ingredients for this "cake" of an effective and productive Christian life. As the Bible says in Galatians 5:13, *Serve one another humbly in love.*

Stir all these together and "bake" them in your life. Verse eight tells us that *if you possess these qualities in increasing measure, they will keep you from being ineffective and unproductive in your knowledge of our Lord Jesus Christ.*

When completely "baked" (in heaven), *You will receive a rich welcome into the eternal kingdom of our Lord and Savior Jesus Christ* (2 Peter 1:11).

Are your pantry shelves full of the supplies needed for your spiritual cake?

FIT 2 B HOLY

The walking of my feet
The talking of my tongue
The thinking of my mind
The work my hands have done
Must be scrutinized
By the eyes
Of God and Christ the Son
For you see
His plan for me
Is holiness
Experienced
And expressed

(1 Peter 1:16)

THINK ABOUT IT

What ingredients are running low in your spiritual pantry? Make out a spiritual "grocery list" asking God to replenish your supply.

Hot Biscuits

2 John 3
Grace, mercy, and peace will be with us, from God the Father and from Jesus Christ the Father's Son, in truth and love. [ESV]

WHEN WE COMMIT OUR LIVES TO GOD, HE GIVES US three special ingredients. Those three ingredients enable us to make something useful and beautiful of our lives.

These ingredients "will be with us." They automatically become ours to have and to use; we don't have to ask God to give them to us. Just like ingredients for baking, these ingredients are ready and available in the cupboards of our spiritual kitchen. They are sitting there waiting for us to open and add to our kitchen projects depending only on what we need to use. My Heavenly Father has given me the whole pantry of products when I put my trust in Jesus as my Savior.

What are these three special ingredients? They are three key elements necessary for good, strong Christian living: grace (the favor of God toward sinners), mercy (compassion shown toward an offender), and peace (a state of harmony between people).

Like the buttermilk, lard, and flour in a recipe for good Southern biscuits, these three ingredients God has given His children, grace, mercy and peace, are the three basic characteristics that separate God's children from the rest of the world. We have them in greater abundance than anyone else around us who is not a born-again child of God, and God has made them available to us at any time, in whatever amount we need.

What is the final result of mixing those three ingredients together? We get tasty biscuits, spiritual "biscuits" that are the result of the activity of grace, mercy, and peace in our lives.

What enhances biscuits once they are baked? Serving them with butter and jam! For our spiritual "biscuits," God has given us the spiritual butter and jam of truth and love. *Grace, mercy, and peace will be with us...in truth and love.* When you walk in the truth, loving God and one another is the natural result. In other words, truth and love go together in your life like butter and jam go together on a hot biscuit.

FIT 4 HIS GRACE

Love transforms your mind
Hope restores your heart
Faith surrounds your soul
God gives a brand-new start

Refrain:
Give God your hope your faith your love
He'll send His grace down from above

Angry bitter thoughts
Failure chasing you
Nipping at your heels
Whatever you may do

God sends His kindness
Goodness gentleness
Waves His mighty hand
Helps you when you stand

(Psalm 42:5)

THINK ABOUT IT

Describe your spiritual "biscuit" recipe. Are you missing any ingredients?

Our Inheritance

Revelation 21:27
Nothing impure will ever enter it, nor will anyone who does what is shameful or deceitful, but only those whose names are written in the Lamb's book of life.

WHEN WE PUT OUR TRUST IN GOD, THE BIBLE PROMises us a reward that is more and better than we could ever imagine. 1 Corinthians 2:9 tells us, *What no eye has seen, what no ear has heard, and what no human mind has conceived—the things God has prepared for those who love him.* Part of that unimaginable reward is heaven, as described in the book of Revelation, especially graphically in chapter 21.

God has prepared heaven for His children. Verse seven says that heaven is the inheritance of God's children. According to verse 4, it is a perfect place: *He will wipe every tear from their eyes. There will be no more death or mourning or crying or pain.*

Heaven shines with the glory of God (verse 11). It has twelve entrances, each made of a single pearl (verse 21), and each is guarded by an angel, so only what God allows will be able to get in. In addition, the streets of heaven are paved with pure gold. Verse 21b explains, *The great street of the city was of gold, as pure as transparent glass.*

The Bible pictures heaven as a huge city surrounded by a wall with a special kind of foundation, one made of twelve kinds of precious jewels. Jewels would make the best, most durable of foundations because of their hardness and durability, indicating to us that this city, heaven, will last forever. In 1 Corinthians 3:11, God's Word declares, *For no one can lay any foundation other than the one already laid, which is Jesus Christ.* Our faith in Jesus and His sacrifice on the cross for us is our solid foundation, both for living here on earth *and* for spending eternity with God in the perfect and beautiful heaven He has prepared for those who love Him.

If we have put our faith and trust in God and have received Jesus as our Savior, this is our inheritance...and what a fabulous inheritance it is!

FIT 4 NO MORE

Heaven – the place of No More

No more death
No more dying
No more mourning
No more crying

No more pain
No more tears
No more sorrow
No more fears

(Revelation 21:4)

THINK ABOUT IT

Imagine God writing a will that describes your inheritance. What will it say?

About the Authors

JO ANN RETIRED AS A SEMINARY LIBRARIAN, HAVING previously served as a missionary and Bible teacher. She has been journaling thoughts from her daily devotional times for many years and uses her journaling to write outlines for Bible studies. These devotional thoughts are summaries of a few of those Bible study outlines.

Russ is a retired quality engineer who has been writing poetry for almost all of his life, often writing in response to his Bible reading and meditation. Most of his poems are a reflection on the need to grow consistently stronger in one's Christian walk, reflected in the theme of fitness in the poem titles. In recent years, he has used his poetry to develop a ministry of encouragement by way of email. He writes almost every day and, on some days, more than one poem!

Russ and Jo Ann are both transplanted "Yankees" who have lived more than half their lives in the South, making them "Southerners by choice," as Russ likes to put it. They live in Lexington, South Carolina.

CPSIA information can be obtained
at www.ICGtesting.com
Printed in the USA
LVHW050017261120
672694LV00033B/931

9 781632 219862